GRIEF SUCKS ... BUT LOVE BEARS ALL THINGS

How Grief Tore Me Apart and Put Me Back Together

Gayle Taylor Davis

Quill
Driver
Books

Fresno, California

Published by Quill Driver Books
An imprint of Linden Publishing
2006 South Mary Street, Fresno, California 93721
(559) 233-6633 / (800) 345-4447
QuillDriverBooks.com

Quill Driver Books and Colophon are trademarks of
Linden Publishing, Inc.

ISBN 978-1-61035-195-9

Printed in the United States of America
on acid-free paper.

Library of Congress Cataloging-in-Publication Data
on file with the Library of Congress

MIX
Paper from
responsible sources
FSC® C011935

Contents

For Tony, who taught me that love has a beginning but no end.

The Gathering

I spend the day gathering pain,
pulling a tuft of sorrow here,
a twig of despair there.

If truth be told, I spend my
nights in the harvest, too.

Like an anxious farmer,
I work fervently,
hoping to gather my crop,
then lay it at your feet and say,

"There, God,
I'm done."

Preface

The power of words is what I've spent my life's work helping teenagers to understand, but when my husband died unexpectedly, my students taught me something that they had known all along. Finding the right word for exactly the right emotion or situation doesn't always require a thesaurus. While some words might be more eloquent or evocative, any teen can tell you that there are simple, all-purpose words that can pretty much sum up a variety of bite-you-in-the-ass life situations.

From teenagers, I learned that when life kicks you in the teeth with some terrible disaster, "That sucks!" pretty much nails it. So when your husband of 32 years dies unexpectedly, and a group of 15-year-olds surrounds you, patting you gently on the shoulder and whispering, "We're so sorry, Mrs. Taylor. That totally sucks!" you know that in their own way they understand the bitterness and betrayal of loss. In that moment, with that perfect word, they have reached across age and authority and held your heart in theirs … and knowing that someone else understands and cares is the first step in surviving.

WARNING: This is not a book about the stages of grief along with suggestions on how to cope with those stages. I bought many of those books, some of them good, but if that is what you are looking for, put this book down. Those books talked to me in generalities: denial, bargaining, anger, acceptance, etc. I couldn't picture those in my head, couldn't grasp how they looked in real life. So think of this book as the guy on the corner with his trench coat opened wide as he whispers, "Pssst! Want to see what grief looks like?"

This is my grief. Gut-wrenching, ass-kicking grief. I didn't think I could survive it, but I did. I share it with you, so that you might understand that you are not alone. You are not crazy, although at times you may feel that way. You are grief-stricken. In the early stages, you may wonder how you will survive, but because you are searching for a way, I know that you will find one.

I am sharing this very private experience with you because I understand what you're going through. Boy, do I ever! I know that you will come through grief a changed person, one who is stronger than you might have thought possible.

1

In the Beginning ...

It was just an ordinary Thursday afternoon.

And then it wasn't.

APRIL 21, 2005

7:00 A.M.

I am a wife.

"Do you want a cup of coffee to go?" I ask. Your look of mock disbelief makes me smile. I am teasing. I already have it poured in your to-go cup. I gather up my book-bag, purse, and ID, and you offer to drive me to work today. I accept.

10:15 A.M.

I am a mother.

Text message during my prep, "Mom, u kno where my car keys r?"

I reply, "Look on the end table by the chair in the family room." (I can't bring myself to use texting lingo.)

"Thx, Mom."

11:05 A.M.

I am a teacher.

"Tell us why we're doing this again, Mrs. T?"

I reply, "We're studying Greek Mythology to learn the research process. Plus, we get to learn about the Greeks and what they believed. Exciting! Right?"

"Gr-o-a-a-a-n-n-n!"

4:25 P.M.

I am a widow.

I dial your office for the fourth time. A strange voice finally comes on the line, asking, "Who is this?"

Startled, I demand, "Who are you, and why are you answering my husband's phone?"

"This is Officer Jeffers of the Clovis Police Department. Ma'am, do you have someone there with you?"

"No—what has happened?" Suddenly, there is a knot the size of Texas in my gut.

"Ma'am, is there someone you can call to be with you?"

"Ma'am?"

In the beginning ... there is the end. The end of normal. The end of security and comfort. The end of you and me. It's like a horrific accident that I don't want to see, yet I can't avoid.

So here I am, spirited away by friends and coworkers to your office, to the police, and to you. I want to turn and run, to avoid the horror of what awaits, but I let myself be led into your office. What I see surprises me. There you are in the waiting room, asleep on the sofa. My heart quickens in hope, and then I see your arm flung carelessly off the edge. It is purple and mottled. But your face, your sweet face, has such peace. I touch you and know. There is almost a little smile on your face, and my first thought is to thank God that you didn't suffer. Suddenly I can't bear to think of the people who will take you now, who will treat you as just another body, just another job to do. Not when you are so vulnerable and alone. I can't bear to think of them standing over you and chatting about their plans for the weekend or how their team is doing.

WAITING …

Death took you mid-sentence
Your mouth a perfect little "o,"
as if caught by surprise,
and I, too, leaned forward,
waiting for your reply,
and when none came.
I kissed your back, your face,
your hands,
praying God's blessing on your soul,
praying the hands that would take you
would know you were a child of God
and lift you gently home.

Sometimes I lean again,
waiting, my mouth a perfect little "o,"
as if caught by surprise,
waiting for your reply
until I am struck deaf
by the echoing silence.

The police and coroner converge with questions. But I am in deep water, arms and legs flailing, trying to tread, so only fragments come to me. " … foul play … don't know … any cash … office … natural …" Suddenly, I am wrung dry, sitting calmly in the chair across from your desk. But it is the police officer in your chair. He is explaining, "Ma'am, until we know what happened, we have to treat this as a crime scene. Did your husband keep any cash in his office?"

"No," I tell him, and explain that we went to lunch and you had cash in your wallet. If someone had robbed you, wouldn't they have taken that, I ask. He checks your wallet. It seems to assure him, and the coroner takes his place. She has a plastic bag. She places your wallet, your watch, and your wedding ring inside. "I'm supposed to log these in," she says. She looks at my face, which doesn't feel like my face, and then hands the bag across the desk to me. "But, I think it would be all right for you to take these with you." I clutch the bag to my chest like a life vest.

Then they wrap you in white plastic for transport. They leave only your face exposed, which seems strange until I realize they did this for me. Had they covered your face, I wouldn't have been able to breathe. How smart of them to know that.

My friends take me home. More and more friends converge. We tell my daughter, and her impulse is to run. I hold her tight. She has her grief, and I have mine. I call my oldest daughter in Texas; her grief wrenches itself in deep sobs across the miles. I am stricken that I cannot hold her. My friends, bless them, gather at the dining room table. They organize and plan. I wander the house and finally stand at the front window, gazing out. I am in the water again, floating just underneath the surface. Occasionally, a friend will swim down and ask a question. I nod and bubbles lift skyward. The friend retreats.

From the kitchen, I hear a friend on the phone. "Can you prescribe something so she can sleep? She just lost her husband." His voice becomes impatient, then pleading. "Okay, call it in. I will go pick it up." His conversation sounds hushed and urgent. I suddenly realize that he's talking about me.

I am floating again. A friend brings something on a plate. "Here, take a bite," she says. "You have to eat." Obediently, I open my mouth. I float away again. I hear their voices from the dining room and the murmur has an odd, womb-like feel to it. It feels comforting. The drugs arrive. I hate drugs, but tonight I take the glass of water and the little white pill. I swallow and let it float down my throat. I am on my back in the bed, which seems unusually large. I wonder how I will survive without you.

Then there is nothing.

THE SECRET OF SCOTTISH DOOKS

I always wondered how they did it,
those Scottish Dooks who dive into the icy waters
on New Year's Day.

And why they would want to mystified me,
as I have spent my life running from pain
until it dragged me, kicking and screaming, head first
into the icy brink.

And then I learned their secret ... and I will tell you
what I learned, so when death drags you under,
you will know what to expect ...
Oh, it won't make it any easier,
But at least it won't catch you by surprise.

So here it is—the secret to surviving the icy water.
They don't feel anything at first—
and neither will you.

When they tell you your loved one is dead, deceased, expired,
your entire body will suddenly go from 98.6 degrees normal
to a tingly, frozen popsicle in the time it takes you to hang up
the phone.

Suddenly you will be surrounded by friends and loved ones,
like the Dooks frolicking in the icy surf, emerging toward those
on the beach
holding towels and smiling broadly at their folly.

But what you don't see, what the news camera never records,
is that once home,
after their friends have gone, and the cameras are turned off,
body heat returns, one molecule at a time,

each molecule a memory, a searing, burning reminder that
you're still alive.

And they never warned you, all those years ago, when you
promised until death do us part,
that they would rip him from your body, one cell, one searing
memory at a time,
and that, unlike giving birth, "giving death" has no joy,
only immeasurable pain.

And the Dooks still mystify me, why they return year after year,
to plunge into that icy water, unless, they, like me,
are seeking to find peace in the numbing cold.

I awake with a nasty taste in my mouth and, in my first coherent
moment, I remember. The pain is like in those old movies where they are
building a railroad, and the men hit a spike with a sledge. Except the spike
is placed just left of center on my chest. I want to cry out, but the pain is
so great there is only a gasping, empty wail.

Later I will understand that sleep is a black forgetfulness and morning
is a red-hot remembering.

2

The Funeral

My principal gives my three closest friends time off to be with me. This is a kind thing, a necessary thing. I am a nonfunctioning unit of human miasma. They call me. "We're picking you up at 9:00 A.M." Somewhere within, the bodily functions, like breathing, kick in and rote memory skills resurface, allowing me to shower and get ready. I wait like a little girl in grade school waiting for her school bus.

Downtown is quaint, with antique stores tucked in among old homes turned into businesses. The funeral home sits on a corner across from the optometrist's office. It is a large, Tudor style building looming over a small, Hansel-and-Gretel storybook house to its left. We used to joke that you should buy that little house next to the funeral home for your accounting/tax business, and we would put a sign out front saying, "The only sure thing in life is death and taxes. Your choice!" Our little joke seems ironic now. Not so funny since a heart attack took you from me.

I've never been inside before. My body is repelled by my having to be here. It begins to tremble and my hands shake uncontrollably. I excuse myself to the lady's room. I do the necessaries, and then splash water on my face. "Get a grip! Get a grip!" I scold myself. And then the worst happens. I get the giggles. Nothing is funny. NOTHING! But I can't control myself. I pinch myself hard on the arm. It helps.

A tisket, a tasket, don't make me choose a casket,
My husband's gone, my mind's all wrong,
Just throw me in a basket …

This old rhyme pops into my head, all twisted and perverted. My mind can't stop singing it. I try to smile into the mirror. It looks more like a grimace, but it will have to do. I join my friends again. The lady comes to help us. She has a kind smile, and I can tell she has done this more than once, so I begin to relax a little and allow myself to breathe. She takes all the pertinent information and then ushers us into the showroom.

I can't believe it. I'm shopping for a casket. I look at my friends. We four are the inveterate shoppers of the world. We can shop T.J. Maxx, Macy's, and HomeGoods until we bring them to their knees. Can we actually be shopping for a casket for you? My beloved, sweet, southern boy of a man? You, with the gentle heart and tender mercies? I am shocked into submission and have to get serious about a choice. Some are gaudy, metallic monstrosities. Some are downright ugly. But there is one, a handsome, hand-hewn wooden casket, that seems do-able. If I have to give you up to the earth, this one, carved and polished like an old antique, seems to be the only choice.

I choose a plot. There was a question of cremation, but I remembered your dream of five acres in the country and the look on your face when it became ours. This is the last gift I can give you, this piece of ground near towering pines. This will be yours.

The choices are made, and the day comes that I must give you up to the earth. There is the military pomp and circumstance, the playing of taps, the handing over of the flag. These are your right as a decorated veteran of war, a recognition of your bravery and courage under fire. These are qualities I lack. I am frightened beyond understanding. My brain has checked out. I can barely walk without support. Is this what it feels like to be a coward?

We have the Celebration of Life at the Veteran's Memorial Hall. Friends, loved ones, clients of yours, all speak to your goodness on this earth. I am so frightened to not have you with me that I am disconnected. It's as if I am one of those people the police find, lost and wandering, with no memory of who they are. I go to the lady's room, and when I exit I have completely lost my bearings. I don't know which way will take me back to your celebration. Fear rises like bile in my throat. I go back into the restroom and hide in a stall, crying and hyperventilating. Eventually, friends find me and lead me back to where I belong.

And then the ceremonies are over. Friends leave, as they must, and grief, a sorry bastard, kicks my ass while I'm already down and defenseless.

I realize I have a lot to learn.

3

The University of Sorrow

It surprises me that I am ignorant. I have a BA in English and a Lifetime Teaching Credential, yet I know little to nothing about grief. Like a good student, I purchase books and search the Internet. I attend a grief group. To be honest, I don't find them helpful. They are like words in some obscure poem that can only be understood by experience. Grief has a language all its own.

VOCABULARY 101

You've been gone five months
and twenty-eight days.
I, who never balanced a checkbook,
have become an accountant of the
days spent without you.

And I enrolled in Vocabulary 101,
a crash course,
I think I'm getting an "A."

Denial didn't take long,
even though I clung to it
with hopeful, questioning eyes.
They spelled it out for me
with lightning-bolt speed,

then drove the meaning home with the thud
of soft earth on your coffin.

I nailed **grief** in the first month,
took its gory little definition home, let
it chew on my heart and spit it out,
raw, throbbing, mush for guts.
Yes, I've definitely nailed that one.

Sorrow, now that one was messy,
kept dripping down my face,
ruining my mascara,
memories disguised as tears,
sneaky little fellow too, he keeps coming back
for relearning.

Lost took a little longer,
kept confusing it with directions,
like north and south,
until some guy in a blue pickup
flipped me the bird and yelled,
"Hey, lady, where the hell do you
think you're going?" and I realized,
I didn't know,
I couldn't see my future without you.

Loss could be confused with **lost**,
except it's so much more tangible,
like when you put something
really valuable in your pocket, and then
when you reach in to get it, it's not there,
panic and dread rise up to your throat,
loss is that sinking feeling
when you know it's gone—forever.

Longing is hard to wrap your brain around
because, although it says it's a noun,
it feels like a verb, even without the helping
verb **am**,
it pulls at your chest, a great aching desire,
reaching for the one thing you cannot have
like a giant rubber band pulled to its breaking point

Acceptance, now that one's a tough one.
I keep tearing up the card and they keep
placing it back on my desk,
telling me I won't pass the class
until I learn it.

I pick up the newest card, crumple it into a little
ball and toss it toward the garbage can where
it bounces off the rim and rolls to the teacher's feet.
He picks it up, uncrumples it, then places it in front of me.
He gives me a stern look, sighs deeply, then plods out the door,
letting it swing shut behind him.
I stare at the card in disgust
then yell at the door, loud enough for him to hear me,

"I hate this class!"

A stranger in a foreign land is lost. And so, I am lost. Death takes a perverse stand in educating the lost. First step: total immersion. I am fluent now. I speak grief. And as any traveler knows, the first step in navigating a foreign land is to master the language.

The best thing about being fluent is that now, when I get mad at Grief, I can tell him off in his own language.

I learned a lot in college: math, science, history, economics, and literature. What finds me now are the writers, the poets. I understand better now what they tried to teach me then.

HEMINGWAY'S TRUTHS

And we were young then
and in our garden of Eden,
no thought of loss or sorrow,
each day a moveable feast
of touch and taste and smell,
of devouring each other until
our hearts were satiated and
complete.

Who knew of death in the afternoon,
that snake in the garden, and how it
would bring a farewell to arms that would
hold and comfort and soothe.

In our time of innocence, we thought not to ask
for whom the bell tolls, our only thought to hold
tight to each other, to dream, to breathe.

But even in Eden, the sun also rises,
and what was true at first light is this—
to have and have not is a cruel paradox,
to have memories but not you
is only a perverted joy.

And now, the dangerous summer calls,
and I drift alone and wait,
knowing the fate of the old man and the sea,
and that in the end,
the winner takes nothing.

4

Is It Me or Is It Memorex?

I am in a constant state of telling and retelling what happened to you. In the lunch room, friends ask and I tell. In the classroom, I tell each class what has happened. I do it out of self-defense. They know why I was gone, and when I come back your death is like the elephant in the room, so I tell the story again and again. For five classes.

I see friends in the market. They ask and I tell. One day, at the gas station, a couple comes in while I am paying.

"Say, aren't you Tony's wife?" the man asks. I can't help it. I start to cry, because I am, and yet I'm not. How can I be a wife when I don't have a husband? I tell them the story.

"You went to work, laid down on the sofa in your office, had a heart attack, and died." There it is. All spelled out for everyone.

One day, in the lunchroom, while I am telling the story for the umpteenth time, I hear my voice as though it belongs to someone else, and I realize that I'm sick of hearing it. In the beginning when I told it, there was a sense of wonder in the telling, like, "Can you believe this really happened?" But, now, it is a monotone, rote, boring recitation, sort of like the multiplication tables we recited in elementary school.

1 x 1 is one,
2 x 2 is four,
you minus you is nothing.
Math helps me keep score.

The lesson is not lost on me. They ask, and I learn.

5

The Two Faces of Grief

WHY'D YOU HAVE TO LEAVE IN APRIL?

I used to like April,
But now it just pisses me off,
Like some bitch in high school
Who knows just how to push your buttons.

I have to be honest. I would like to say I am handling this better than I am. That I call up friends when I get lonely, or perhaps invite friends over. But that would be a lie. Here's what I do on a daily basis:

I get up and go to work.
Stay at work late.
Grab a sandwich in town.
Drive around aimlessly until almost dark.
Drive home.

Once I leave the city limits and get on the country roads to our house, I wail. Not some wimpy little kid wails, but these horrible, gut-wrenching wails. They leave me exhausted, my throat raw. But they make me weak and submissive enough to face an empty house. Weak enough to sleep, eventually. I often wonder if other drivers see me, but I am so weary, I don't care. This is no way to live, and I know that. At this point, grief has me against the wall and is pummeling me senseless. All I can do is wail. I am a kettle on the stove, with grief bubbling over until it comes out in this high-pitched wail of sorrow.

My beloved is like a gazelle or a young stag.
Behold, he is standing behind our wall.
He is looking through the windows.
He is peering through the lattice.

—Song of Solomon 2:9

THE WAILING WALL

My heart is a wailing wall,
all that remains of our holy union,
though shattered and broken
from our imposed exile,
its tattered remnants remain
a testament to our love,
and daily I come,
tucking prayers between
the broken parts,
each memory a prayer for what has been,
each tear a prayer for what will be again.

I feel helpless in my grief. Yet in some strange way, there is power in it, too. My wails are a protest against your leaving. They are the wild howl and anger of loss. They are the loss of 32 years of love turned into something tangible. They echo within the confines of my car. They careen wildly through the house. You are gone, but I don't have to like it. During the day, I have to be my old self, the teacher, the one who is calm and in charge. But when night comes, I can be a wild animal, prowling the house and howling in pain and sorrow. I come to understand that my wails are my power against self-destruction.

But this is not the face I show the world. When friends and co-workers ask how I'm doing, I say, "Okay." I never say "great" because that would be a lie too big to profess. But, "okay" is acceptable. They buy it. At work, my students come in and we focus on the work at hand or talk about what's going on in their lives. But during my prep period, I lock the classroom door and I lie on the floor behind my desk and weep. Before the next class arrives, I clean up the mess my mascara has made on my face and start again. Smile. *Okay.*

HOW TO FIX THINGS

Broken china: gather all the scattered pieces, dull, shale-like chips; pretend it is a jigsaw puzzle, squeeze glue generously, place back in cupboard, hope no one notices.

Broken lamp: buy new bulb and shade, use small wrench to tighten bolt, place upright on table, tell person who's mad it needed refurbishing anyway.

Busted leg: act tough, go to emergency room, apply warm plaster over soft wrap, wait 6-8 weeks, milk it for all it's worth.

Broken cd: throw in trash, go to FYE, look in used section, buy it, bring it home, place it in cd player. Enjoy.

Broken heart: get up and breathe, plaster smile on face, when asked anything, say, "I'm okay." Lie on the floor and cry until your mascara turns your ears black. Get up each morning and repeat.

6

The Road Is Paved with Good Intentions

As the old saying goes, the road to hell is paved with good intentions. So is the road to heaven. There is almost no way to avoid the good intentions of friends. I don't blame them. What do you say when someone has lost so much? A lot of friends avoid me for this very reason. They don't know what to say and fear saying the wrong thing. They really shouldn't worry. They are going to say the wrong thing eventually. They can't help it. The wrong thing can be almost anything if it is said at the wrong time. And how can they be expected to know that?

What they need to know is that it's not them; it's me. It's as if I am burned over one hundred percent of my body, and no matter how they try to help, if they reach out to touch me, it's going to hurt. So I think of my friends, now, as doctors in attendance. They are specialists. Some attend to my need for food. Others to my need to tell my story again and again. Still others call daily just to let me know they are thinking of me. Their love and concern touches my heart, but it still leaves me raw and aching.

Other friends, in their innocence, offer platitudes, the kind that make me crazy. I have come to understand, though, that even this has a purpose. When they touch a nerve, it forces me to deal with it—to think about that particular piece of pain and to find a way to understand what it has meant to me, and in some weird way to embrace it. This forces me to understand that particular pain came from a place of love, and to understand that leads me to a place of gratitude for having had that love in my life.

SWEETER THAN CHOCOLATE

A well-meaning friend told me,
as we sat eating chocolate cheese cake one evening,
"From now on, this will be your sex – chocolate!
Chocolate cake, chocolate ice cream, chocolate cheese cake!"
We both smiled as we licked the Oreo-crusted crumbs from our
forks.

I didn't tell her that I dream about you, about sex. We are young
again,
racing up the stairs, taking two at a time in our joy,
shedding clothes as we run,
like kids racing toward the swimming hole,
each wanting to be first to jump heart-long into our bed,
laughing, moaning, panting, wriggling to the surface
until we both emerge, faces damp and smiling in the dark.

And so I lick the fork, until no crumbs remain,
and look at her and smile
until I think my heart will break.

Until she made this comment, I hadn't actually thought about sex in
terms of grief. Grief was just this big ball of pain. Had the doctor asked
me, I couldn't have pin-pointed one place in particular where it hurt
more than another. My friend forced me to think about it. To mourn the
intimacy we shared. To understand that it was a finite and particular loss.
It shocked me at first, but she did me a favor. I began to understand that
grief was made up of all the little parts of my life with you that were lost
when you died. I would need to address these to understand how to deal
with that loss.

And so I remember our intimacy. I cry at first. There are so many precious moments. But I remember that day in the woods. I embrace it. I relive it. During college you were a logger in the summers. One day you took me up the hill to watch you fell a tree. I remember.

THE WOODSMAN

"How do you fell a tree?" I asked.
"Oh, dangerous work!" you replied.
"You need a chain saw the size of a man,
an axe, a sledge, and wedge to
drop it in the right direction.

"You have to size up the tree, check for knots
that might choke your saw.
Here, let me show you."

And so you did. With a dancer's grace
you skirted the tree, checking with a practiced eye
for things that could go awry.
Hefting your axe, you cut a delicate "V" in its underbelly,
then ripped the cord on your saw, turning the soft forest
into a raging beast,
the giant Cedar split the sky, screaming, then
landed with a thundering belch!

You looked at me and grinned
as the ground shook beneath our feet,
then came close and nuzzled my cheek,
"How do you fell a woodsman?" you asked.
"Oh, dangerous work!" I replied.

"You need a heart the size of a woman,
tender words, gentle kisses, and love to
drop him in the right direction.

"You have to size up the man, check for unspoken needs
that might choke your love.
Here, let me show you."

And so I did. With a dancer's grace
I skirted you there, checking your face and your heart
for needs that could go awry.
Hefting my heart, I kissed a delicate "V" on your underbelly,
then pulled the snap on your jeans, turning the soft forest
into a raging beast,
slicing your heart from behind, so you almost didn't see it
coming.

The Woodsman split the sky, screaming, then
landed with a thundering sigh.
You looked at me and grinned
as the ground shook beneath our love.

I came close and nuzzled your cheek,
"And that's how you fell a woodsman!" I said.
"Dangerous work!" you replied.

Every sweet memory brings up a time of sorrow in the remembering.
The joy of memory is wrestled to the ground by sorrow.

WIDOWMAKER

Every logger knows the danger,
it's not the falling tree that will get you,
any logger worth his salt is smart enough
to steer clear of that.

But the danger lies in what you can't see,
somewhere, toward the innocent sky,
lodged in the top of a tree,
a widowmaker waits.

A broken limb, a chunk of a giant cedar,
coughed up as the giant falls through its friends.
They hold it, waiting, as if for revenge
until the unsuspecting logger is given the all clear.

And then, when the roar of the bucker's saw breaks their silence,
they hurl it, the forest holding its breath
until it finds its mark, an eye for an eye,
a limb for a limb,
nature's retribution.

For 32 years, I held my breath,
a blink of an eye in timber years,
but still, they got you.
And I,
I stand with the trees of the forest
and weep.

7

The Longness of Days

It's funny, not in a ha-ha way, but rather in a weird way, how long the days seem since you have gone. We got married, got jobs, had children, and those days were like tipped dominoes, falling so fast it seemed like we were 25 and then we were 50. Even as we lived them, I mourned how quickly our girls grew up and how the time seemed to get away from us. But the days now remind me of that sticky curl of paper we used to catch flies on. I wonder now about the poor flies. Did they hang up there by the ceiling, looking down at life passing them by? Did they yell at their friends, "Hey! It's me. I'm stuck up here. Hey! Somebody help me!" Some days that's how I feel. Stuck. Helpless.

SHOO-FLY HUMBLE CRY

I remember the fly now,
With guilt and not pleasure,
And how we hung that sticky
Curl of paper high against the
Ceiling, twisting, beckoning with
Its pungent, sickening smell,
And how he bought it,
Hook, line, and stinker,
Placing his dainty little fly feet into
That treacherous goo, and how
We thought not of him at all,

Or how his fly wife would miss
Him at dinner, and then
Search all their fly haunts,
Growing too weak to flutter
Until we found her dead in the
Windowsill from sorrow and grief,
And, with careless unconcern
How we dusted her off to be thrown
In the trash.
And did he suffer I wonder,
And watch from high on
His death perch,
And call out, unheeded,
"Help me, I'm here!"

And then I remember that days are made of hours, and hours of minutes, and minutes of seconds. I can't control days right now, perhaps, but I can control seconds and minutes. For these next few minutes I can read this article. Or I can clean the kitchen. Or I can call a friend. And for these minutes I won't be wracked with sorrow or pain. These minutes, added together, can become an hour. An hour that will not find me dwelling in memory and sorrow, but one that will find me engaged in the living of the moment of this day.

Then I think back to that old children's story, now long forgotten, and I wonder. How was it that Alice got out of that rabbit hole?

FREAKIN' FRIDAYS

Sometimes it's only certain parts of the day that wear me down. During working hours I am most at peace. It is regimented. Bells ring. Students pass. Papers demand to be graded. There is enough distraction that I can more easily survive there. But I can't live at work. The truth is, I can't live at home, either. Not in the sense of a real life. Grief has turned home on its head. What used to be my sanctuary has become a lion's den. Each time I return home, I do battle with what used to be and what can never be again. I'm telling you now, no little slingshot and rock can change the reality of never seeing you again.

Years ago, Friday nights were cool. It was the end of the work week, time to relax and play. A whole world of possibilities opened before us that wouldn't close until Sunday night. Would we go to the movies? Out to dinner? Rent a movie and stay home and snuggle?

Fridays now are "Freakin' Fridays." Long before the 2:40 bell rings on Friday afternoon, my heart is digging in its heels, wanting to be dragged anyplace else but into Friday night.

Friday night. It's an exclamation point! An underscore. It's boldface type. The message is always clear. You're not freakin' here. You aren't at your office! You're not waiting for me in the parking lot. You're not at home on the tractor or in your workshop. You aren't stopping by my mom's.

No matter how much I long to put my hands on your dear, sweet face, look into your dark brown eyes and tell you I missed you today—you're never freakin' here!

So Fridays, they're killers. I don't know how I survive them. It's like throwing my heart out on the freeway in five o'clock traffic and letting semis use it for target practice. What I get home with is a beat-up, mush-for-brains, torn apart heart.

Maybe I can convince the government to do away with Fridays. Or maybe there's a magic pill that can let me sleep through until Sunday. Or maybe Scotty can beam me up.

I just wish Freakin' Fridays would leave my heart alone. If you talk to me on a Friday night, I am not responsible for what comes out of my mouth. Who knows what a person might say when their heart is being ripped to shreds.

Changing location doesn't make the days any shorter. Trust me. I went to New York, a long way from California, but I took you with me. Long days. Longer nights.

SOUS CHEF

I found my heart yesterday,
scattered and broken upon
the rocks at Central Park.

So, I picked it up and molded
it like silly putty into what
I thought would suffice.

Then took it home again and
baked it in a low oven at 225°
for an hour.

But, still, it doesn't work—
hard as a rock!
At 57, I've forgotten
how to cook.

IN A NEW YORK MINUTE

New York with(out) you,

Walking down Broadway,
I carry you with me in the rolled up cuff of my sleeve
so at a moment's notice I can pull you out
and suck you deep into my lungs
to feel your sweet breath hot against mine.

Or sometimes I tuck you nonchalantly
into the back pocket of my jeans and
ride with you on the N train to Coney Island,
where we watch Miss Electra shoot sparks
from her tongue, and in the warmth of the
Freak Show theater I can feel your heat
like a tender caress against my ass.

When hunger pains strike, I take you with
me to the Palace Diner, where I seat you
in the chair opposite, and my eyes
devour your face, watching for your
crooked smile, our eyes melting together
until we are tethered like two spacewalkers
suspended in the universe.

And later, when the New York night falls,
muggy and warm, I stuff you underneath
my pillow where I can feel your soft breath
tickle my neck as we spoon, and I dream
with your warm hands cupped tenderly
around my breasts.

But in the morning, when the sun pokes
his surly head in the room like some Brooklyn
cop trying to get me to confess that you are gone,
I take your memory, fold it like an origami crane,
tuck you back inside my heart and tell him I'm not
talking until I get me a lawyer.

8

Material Girl

You are gone, and all that remains are memories. And, of course, your things. The truck you drove. The books you read. The clothes you wore. Suddenly, these *things* become disproportionately signifi-cant because they are the only tangible proof that you existed. They are suddenly all I *have* of you.

You have this lined, flannel shirt that you wore when the days were cold. I drag it around with me like Linus's blanket. I sleep in it. It's comforting in a way that's hard to explain. Just knowing that your arms were in those sleeves makes it feel somehow like you are holding me when I wear it. I wanted to wear it to your funeral, but I didn't want my friends to know how crazy and obsessed I have become.

I found a polo shirt that you had thrown on the chair in the bedroom. It smells of you. That sweet, musky smell of your cologne and the essence of you. At night, in bed, I bury my face in it. When I close my eyes, it keeps me from sheer panic. I hide it in the closet each morning to keep it safe. I am one sick material girl.

Suddenly, I am Madonna—without the great body. No voice either. Just the crazy desire for things. Your things. Your shirts. Your socks. Your boots. Especially your boots.

The thing that breaks my heart the most is your boots. They are not some fancy, stitched leather cowboy boots with swirls and flair. They are simple, humble, everyday work boots. They sit by your chair in the family room. I'm afraid to move them. My brain pretends that if I leave them there, you will come back. It's like your things and I are holding our breath, waiting for your return.

YOUR OLD BOOTS

I finally moved your old boots
from where they stood by the chair
in the family room.

I kept them there for months,
pretending that you were out
in the workshop
and would be coming in
momentarily.

And you would sit in the chair,
taking off your slippers, and
we would talk as you
pulled your boots on,
about anything and nothing,
just enjoying each other's company,
then you would be off to ride the tractor.

But the longer they sat there,
the more brazen the lie became,
until I finally moved them
into the laundry room.

There I can pretend that you
are off on the boat,
sailing with friends, but
will soon come back,
sunburned and smiling,
telling me you came in
first, or second,
or any place at all.

In the clutter of the laundry room
they are not so glaring,
and some days I have to dig them
out so they don't disappear entirely,
and some days I pull them on
and clomp around in your size 10
boots, with my size 6 feet lost
in the soft, wrinkled, cordovan leather.

Their weight and heft feel clumsy
and awkward, and I struggle to
find my balance, until I squat,
folding my arms around the boot-tops
and bury my head in my knees,
knowing what it's like to walk without you
for the very first time.

Eventually, my brain understands that these material things that I hold on to will not bring you back. I realize that, at first, this attachment is a necessary thing. It gives me something of you to hold on to when I am floundering and scared. When I am stronger, I begin letting them go. I clean out your side of the closet. I fill its emptiness with some of my clothes.

The metaphor does not escape me. The gaping hole inside of me must be filled with more of my things, too. My challenge is to find what more there is of me without you.

9

The Guilt-o-Meter

I've always heard about karma biting you in the ass, and it came to me after you died that maybe this horrible pain of your loss was payback for every mean thing I ever did or said. That somehow I deserved this, or worse yet, maybe my failings as a human being were the cause of your death. I began to worry that maybe I hadn't been the kind of wife to you that I should have been. I began to second-guess everything that had been our life. *Bad wife*, I thought. *Bad, bad wife*! I could see this big red stamp on my forehead—"Guilty!" It's a weird, freaky feeling, but I've come to understand that grief doesn't think logically.

DORIAN GRAY'S PICTURE

That sordid story of Wilde's lodged in my mind all these years,
like a chunk of raw meat waiting to be dislodged by the Heimlich.
Your leaving popped it out and left me gasping for breath.

Now, daily, I see deterioration in the mirror, one line at a time,
a crevice of pain across my once smooth forehead,
a bulge below each eye, tattooed with the feet
of a million ancient crows.

I gaze at the image in the mirror and wonder, what is my sin,
that I grow old before my eyes?
Is it that I cannot let grief go,
sending it on its way, like a truculent salesman
who has overstayed his welcome at my door?

Or is my sin that I couldn't save you,
that I ignored what I should have seen,
the color in your face, the once vibrant step
lounging languidly on the couch—
had I become a sinful, irresponsible wife?

Or is it that you were all the goodness in my life,
the outward appearance of all my joys,
the tender, giving lover,
the fixer, the protector,
the one in whose eyes my beauty found voice?

And, now,
now that you are gone,
what remains
is this one dimensional image
that grows older each day
until I am nothing but peeling,
crackling paint
upon a dying canvas.

There is a voice in my head called Grief. He wants me to be in charge of all that goes wrong with the world. He wants me to feel guilty for losing you. Why would he want to heap more pain on me when I am already suffering so? He's a dirty, rotten, little bastard—that's why. It's like he's picked up a snow-globe of the world, shaking it until everything is topsy-turvy, then turns to me and says, "See what you've done?"

But that's not reality. Grief is a liar. A big fat one. He distorts things, messes with my brain, and wants me to take responsibility for things that are not my fault. But, like any liar, he can't change the truth. The truth is, you and I had a wonderful life. We were good for each other. You were a good husband, and I was a good wife. Your dying cannot change that.

So when Grief opens his big, fat, lying mouth, trying to lay the blame for your death at my feet, I tell him to close his pie-hole and, in no uncertain terms, to, "Shut the f**k up!"

10

The Barometer of Sorrow: Cloudy with a Chance of Pain

I have come to realize that I am not alone in my grief. The world mourns you, too. There was a particular goodness about you that the world needed. You were ever the Good Samaritan, the example to others of how goodness creates a more beautiful world. Mired in my own grief, wallowing in tears and pain, I begin to notice a dramatic change in the weather. It's as though she is a two-year-old again, pitching a huge tantrum, stomping her feet until the earth rumbles and shakes, then throwing herself full force to the ground, screaming and crying until she collapses into gale force wails.

For some reason, this wild weather comforts me. It validates my sorrow.

Hurricane Weather

The world is all akilter with you gone,
as if it has slipped off its axis,
a whirligig twirling madly out of control.

Hurricanes whip the east coast,
earthquakes topple lives across the globe,
rains flood cities across the nation.
You didn't leave unnoticed.

In the thrust of your leaving,
my world spins out of control,
first, frozen in fear and grief,
now engulfed by a flood of
words, pouring forth from a levee
burst by pain.

Each day brings a new disaster
as you pour from my life,
a trickle of lost glances,
a torrent of lost hugs and warm embraces
a deluge of lost dreams and hopes,

until hurricane winds strike full force,
leaving me so much flattened debris,
my love trickling out, staining the page
like lonely kisses on discarded tissue.

11

One Ringy-Dingy ...

More than anything, I long to talk to you, to hear your voice. To suddenly be separated from you and know that I can never tell you how much I love you, or gripe about a bad day at work, or ask what you want for dinner, is just unbearable. Without thinking, I pick up the phone and dial your office and then, suddenly, I remember—you are not there. It is shocking. Out of desperation, I do the one thing that can save my sanity. I write you letters. On my computer, I blather on and on, telling you what's in my heart, things I didn't get to say. Sometimes they are angry, but more often they are sorrow-filled. Even though you can't answer, it feels as though we are talking. It saves me. You save me. As months go by and I look back at what I've written, I see myself heal.

December 2, 2005

Dear Tony,

Here it is, already December. It seems impossible that you've been gone over seven months. When this month ends, it will begin a year that we will never share. There will be no us in the years to come, and even just typing that makes me incredibly sad. I miss your sweetness and your goodness. I never knew anyone as kind and loving as you. You always thought of others first. You never looked for the bad in people or said bad things about people. I still can't imagine my life without you. I so want to come home to you.

I wish you could see the house and how it is looking since it was painted and some clean up was done around it. There is much more to do, but you would be so proud of it.

Life is difficult and challenging without you. You would laugh if you could see me lugging those 40 pound bags of pellets into the house. But God is good and has given me some peace at times. I hope that heaven is all that we ever imagined and that you are happy up there with all your family. Just know that I long to hold you and love you.

—Me:O)

November 20, 2006

Dear Tony,

Each day takes me a little further away from you. Sometimes, like today, I can almost imagine, for an instant, you are sitting next to me in the car or are lying next to me in bed. For that instant, there is such incredible sweetness. In the next instant, there is such unbearable sorrow and longing for you. In the ice cream parlor today, and then in Bobby Salazar's over by Wal-Mart, I imagine you sitting there with me, like we had done so many times before. The other night, when I went to Lowe's, there were so many couples in there that it just overwhelmed me with loneliness for you. I don't know what your perception is in heaven, but I hope you can see how much you are loved and missed here on earth.

Then, too, I am often overcome with the sorrow that perhaps I wasn't the best wife I could have been. I hope you were happy. I want that more than anything. We had such a sweetness and love between us. One thing I really miss is my sense of safety with you. I always felt that if I were ever in danger, you could come take care of whatever the problem was. I wish so much that I had made an appointment for you with the heart doctor. Why was I going all the time when you are the one who needed it the most. If there was something I could change, that would be it. Also, I hate it that you had to die alone. I know that Jesus was with you, but you know what I mean. I probably would have made it worse with my hysterics and all, but I could have at least told you one more time how much I love you. I could have kissed your sweet face once more when you could still feel it. I often revisit that day, that week. God was so good to give us that last week. How much fun we had, and how much I treasure those moments now.

I don't know what I'm going to do with my life. I am so lost without you. I think about suicide often. I know that's wrong, and I know that I won't do it, but I do think of it often. I even got your gun out of the bedside table one night, but I just don't want to leave my girls with that legacy. Friends are always telling me how strong I am, but they just don't know how hard it is.

I love you and miss you so much.

—Me:-)

These are but two of the many letters I wrote to you. As I look back over them, I know they are nothing more than idle chatter. But when I am writing it feels like a conversation. I feel connected. And for some reason it loosens up the knot in my chest enough so that I can breathe without pain.

And so, I write.

12

The Darktown Cutter's Ball

It's only an arm. It's only a little blood. What can it hurt?

I'm just going to say it. Suicide. That thought creeps into my mind more often than I would like to admit. I have a gun in the bedside drawer. I know how to use it. I have even taken it out of the drawer, felt the weight and coolness in my hand. I tell myself, "This will end my pain." But a voice whispers back, "But what if it doesn't? What if it only makes it worse?" I worry that if I should do such a thing, would that keep me from seeing you again in Heaven? Nothing is worth that risk, I decide. But still, I think about it.

I think about my girls, too. Is that the legacy I would want to leave them with? A mother too weak to withstand what life gives her? It is not. I know this.

But I know this, too: Sometimes the pain is too great for me to bear. One night, I sit on the floor by the bed, rocking back and forth in my pain. I am out of control with pain. It's as if every cell in my body is on fire with pain, and I have absolutely no control over it. I need control. I slap myself in the face. It stings. I do it again, harder. It hurts. I do it again, and again. I stop for a moment. Then I slap again. It is amazing. This is a pain that is specific. It hurts here. On my face. It hurts, but I can control it. I can slap, or I can stop. Pain. No pain. For the first time in months, I am in control of my pain.

I think of my students at school. Some of them are cutters. I know this because they show me their scars. I never understood why they would do such a thing. Now I do. It focuses the pain. It makes this unbearable ache something tangible. It reduces it to a pain I can identify and control.

Control. That is the operative word. I decide to control my other pain. I allow myself to weep and wail for a part of each day, then I tell myself, "Okay, now you're done. Get up and do something. Anything. Exercise. Read." When thoughts of you creep back in, I push them away and save them for later.

Slap. Don't slap. Grieve. Don't grieve. It seems crazy, but it works. I never have to slap myself again.

On bad days, I sometimes think of the gun in the drawer, but I have come to a new understanding. *Grief is the price of love.* If anyone asked me what I would give to have your love in my life, I would say, "Everything." To commit suicide would be like declaring bankruptcy, running out on a debt. It would be like saying you weren't worth it. As hard as this is, even on a bad day, you are worth everything.

As the months go on without you, I realize that how long I spend in grief is a choice. Our life, my old life, is gone. My grief is a way to hang on to it, to you. But a part of me understands that *hanging on* to grief is a death of its own. To *let go* of grief is to leave my old life behind and find a new one. That scares me. But who wants to live in grief forever? I realize that I am in control of that. When I feel strong enough, I can jump into a new life. Or, I can stay here in grief. I have control.

THE JUMPER

13 stories up, her toes hang over the edge,
a delicate balancing act,
and the crowd gathered below, faces upturned
in expectation, wait . . .

From a distance, her body appears to hover,
like a hummingbird at jasmine,
and someone in the crowd whispers,
"Is she gonna jump, or what?"

The truth is, she doesn't know. . .
What brought her here was clarity,
or the need for it.

She doesn't remember the 13 flights of stairs,
doesn't remember the frantic pounding of her heart,
drawn by the need for air by the 10th flight,
she only remembers what sent her here.

She only remembers his leaving
on an ordinary Thursday afternoon,
his last breath taking hers with it,
and what was left of her heart
in the wake that followed.

And then reality, hovering over her
like some crazed EMT,
pounds her chest and yells,
"Breathe, damn you, breathe!"

And when she refuses, there is the gel
and the paddles and the crazed voice again,
yelling, "Stand clear!"
and memory, an electric shock of sorrow,
forces her to gasp in defeat.

And from far away, she hears the voice
again, "She's back, we've got a rhythm,"
and one by one they retreat
and leave her to this life ...

This life that is no life at all without him,
only memories so sweet that they
melt into sorrow at the beat of her heart.

So she stands on the ledge,
toes keeping a delicate balancing act
between longing and fear,
knowing that to stay is to die
and to jump is to live.

But grief keeps her standing on the ledge,
waiting ...
and the voice from the crowd floats up,
louder, impatient ...
"Hey, lady, you gonna jump or what?"

And the truth is, she doesn't know.
But I know one thing,
if she jumps ...
I'm going with her.

13

Ripley's Believe It or ... What?

Grief tests my sanity. It clouds the boundaries between what is real and what I want to believe. It makes me doubt myself. It makes me discount little miracles that God provides. To make sure I understand, God, in His wisdom, provides proof to my friends as well.

It brings me to the understanding that, while God may not give me what I want, which is you back beside me, He does give me what I need. He helps me to understand that you are gone only in the physical sense. You are still here with me, only in a different dimension. Call it Heaven. I always thought Heaven was a far off place, but now I believe that Heaven is wherever God is, and He has been with me through it all.

A QUARTER'S WORTH, PLEASE

I flash back to our preparation for your Celebration of Life. My friend Alice comes to the house to help the girls and I make three framed picture displays. She brings her computer and photo printer and I get the frames. We decide to set things up in the family room, so I thoroughly vacuum the carpet so nothing will get on the pictures. We sit on the floor together, and the girls and I each choose a theme and Alice prints out pictures for us to use.

Only days into your loss, we are still in shock, and our mood jumps crazily from sorrow at knowing you are gone, and then to laughter at the memories the pictures bring. I finish my frame first and hold it up to show the girls and Alice. As they admire my work, my youngest daughter, Brie, asks, "Mom, what is that on the floor by your leg?" I look down, and there on the carpet is a quarter. I pick it up and squeal with delight.

I cry and laugh and point. There on the wall is the map of the United States that you made out of wood. In each state, there is a place for a state quarter from the Denver Mint. Around the edge are places for the state quarters from the San Francisco Mint. These are enclosed in glass. The girls and I, and even Alice, are in shock. You are here with us! This is a sign. It will be the first of many.

I begin finding quarters everywhere. I find them in the car floorboard, in the women's bathroom at school, in an old purse (no other coins—just quarters). When I tell my friends at school, I can see their expression, like, "Yeah, right!" But in their kindness they humor me. One day though, as my friend JoAnn and I are walking to the lunch room at school, another friend waves me over to ask a question. When I return to JoAnn, she is smiling with rather a shocked look on her face, and she holds out a quarter to me. "I know this is meant for you. If you had taken one step forward before you walked over to Sharon, you would have stepped on it." This happens again and again until my friends understand that it is real.

With each one, I know you are letting me know you are still with me.

A ROSE BY ANY OTHER NAME

Being an accountant, tax season is your busiest time of the year. I explain to you how much I miss you during tax season because you work such long hours—so the week after taxes are due, you decide to make sure I get a lot of Tony time. On the weekend, you take me to the casino for lunch. Later in the week we go to our favorite restaurant, The Japanese Kitchen. We go to movies, have dinner out, and have lots of little treats throughout the week. It's just the most glorious week for me because we are having such a good time. On Thursday, April 21st, you insist on taking me to work, and then you pick me up for lunch and take me to our favorite lunch place, Delly Beans. Then, by that afternoon, you are gone.

In the whirlwind that follows, our oldest daughter, Shea, stationed in the Air Force in San Antonio, flies out to be with her sister and me. After the funeral, in the week before Shea has to return, they decide to go with me to all of our favorite places, so I won't have to be alone the first time I go there without you.

At the Japanese Kitchen, we are all pretty somber sitting around the teppanyaki grill until our cook shows up. The girls and I look at each other in shock. On his belt, his name spelled out in cursive—

"T-O-N-Y."

You let us know you are with us. We have to laugh.

As we leave the restaurant, the building nearby is under construction. Someone had tacked a handwritten sign above the door. "Tony's Place." All we can do is shake our heads and smile. We totally get it. You are here with us. Always.

At each place we visit that week, there is a reminder that you are there with us. We get the message.

One potato, two potato ...

When my first Christmas without you arrives, I know it's going to be hard because every book I read and every friend I talk to tells me that it will be. They are right. Fixing Christmas dinner is a challenge. I am at the kitchen sink peeling potatoes and crying. This is the one chore that you always did. For some strange reason, the juice from raw potatoes burns my hands, so you always volunteered to do this for me. But you are not here. I reach in and pull out potato after potato, each one just another reminder that you are gone. I peel and cry. I reach in and pull out another one. I look at it and let out a scream. My daughter, Brie, runs into the kitchen, and from her expression I can see that I have frightened her. "What happened? Did you cut yourself?" she asks. I hold up the potato for her to see. "Oh, my gosh! It's a heart shaped potato!" she yells.

We both jump up and down, and I cry even harder. It is a gift from you. She knows it. I know it. Of all the bags of potatoes, in all the homes in America ... I got the one with your heart.

Please, Mister Postman

During our 32 years together, we were never apart, other than my short visits to see my sister Bobbi in Oregon. That is a good thing. But because we were always together, we never have a reason to write letters to each other. Now that you are gone, this is a problem. I long to have letters. Something from you that I can read and reread. I need to hear your voice again, even if only in a letter. But I have nothing. I bemoan this fact long and loud to my friends. I implore them to write their loved ones a letter at least once a year telling them how much they mean to them. I think it falls on deaf ears. But still, I long for something from you. I dig through drawers and find a couple of Valentines and anniversary cards. They are sweet, but short. I need letters. It's not going to happen. I know.

Now that you are gone, I need to straighten up many loose ends. I get the bill for the storage of your mother's things in Tennessee. I encouraged you to get that stuff packed up and shipped out here, but you just never got around to it. I wonder if you just couldn't bear to deal with the fact that she was gone now, along with your dad. It's been six years since your mom died, too long to be paying for storage. I call her sister and arrange for her to take what she wants, and have her ship what she thinks the girls will want. I pay the bill.

It arrives. A lot of trunks, cedar chests, and boxes. I begin going through them. In the first box is a large black ledger. I open it up and I can hardly believe what is inside. Letters! Letters you wrote to your mom while you were at college. Letters you wrote your mom while you were in Vietnam. A hundred or more letters, all organized by date. Amazing. No one has to tell me that this is divine intervention. This is no coincidence. God heard my cries, and He answered them hundredfold.

I read. And I read. I hear your voice as an 18-year-old. A sweet southern boy, longing for an education, wanting to make it on his own. I read that your dad has lost his job and you have to leave school. I hear the sadness in your words as you try to comfort your parents and tell them that it will be okay.

I read some more. You are a new recruit in the Army. You are a new soldier in Vietnam. You are a war-weary veteran in Vietnam. I can hear it in your words. You are irritated by the jumpiness of the new guy in your unit. You are irritated by the long periods of boredom between battles.

I read and discover you have a poetic heart. I remember these words you wrote to your mom: "I've decided that life is a bridge and death is an archer. The longer you are on the bridge, the more accurate his aim until, finally, he meets his mark. So I've decided to be happy every day that I have."

You were the happiest man I ever knew. In fact, on the picture I made for the Celebration of Life, the inscription read, "Merry-hearted boys make the best men!" Now I know why.

Another letter reads, "When I get home, the first thing I want is to spend 30 minutes hearing girls giggle!" When I read this, I remember how you used to look at me and smile when we heard the girls giggling and laughing in the other room.

These letters are more than I could have ever imagined. If I had letters from our time together, I would only have known you as a husband. From this gift, from these letters, I get to know a Tony I never knew. I get to understand more deeply the husband and father you became.

A miracle.

14

The Red Badge of Squirmage

In spite of the letters and the solace they bring, I discover they are only a minor skirmish in the long battle with grief. And I agree with those who have fought before.

War is Hell!

RAW RECRUIT

Our house is a war zone
and memories the enemy,
they've had decades to
dig themselves in.

Each day is a walk
through a mine field,
I don't know how
I'm still standing
with all the shrapnel
I carry.

They don't honor
Geneva Conventions
or care how they torture.

And when the pain is too much,
some days I taunt them—

Why don't you shoot me already?

You were always my hero. You were brave and strong. You could do anything, except beat death.

After you died, I discovered new heroes. I see them in restaurants. They sit alone. Little white-haired ladies. Or sometimes they sit together. But I admire the ones who sit alone the most. I tell myself, *If they can do it, why can't I?* They are alone. They are smiling, eating, breathing. They have survived loss. They are my heroes.

I have decided that grief is just a boot-camp for wusses. Reality is some leathery drill sergeant in your face, yelling, "Suck it up, you little pussy! Get up and stop your whining!" Me? I'm just some raw recruit, trembling in my boots, tears streaming down my face. And right at this moment, I hate him. But part of me knows that he just wants me to survive, and I can't do that if all I do is whine and cry. So I'm trying my best to stand up straight, give reality the three finger salute, and soldier on.

COURAGE UNDER FIRE

I've never thought of myself as brave.
In fact, if asked, I would have told you
that I am the biggest coward who ever
ran in the opposite direction from danger.

But since you've left, I believe I understand
how heroes are born.
They are born from unavoidable
danger and loss.
When the worst that can happen
has happened,
when you are caught naked in the
crossfire and death takes you prisoner,
that's when heroes are born.
And heroism is always a choice.
Oh, people in the newspaper who've
saved someone from drowning or
from a fire will say, "Oh, I didn't even
think, I just jumped right in!"

But the truth is, there was a moment,
however brief or agonizing, where
a choice was made, to go or to run,
to help or to flee, and the brave heart,
the heroic heart, knows there is really
only one choice.

And when you left with no warning,
I learned something else about heroes.
The world sees only the act, that heroic
deed that has been accomplished.
Only the hero knows how his body
trembled, his heart bled, in the act,
how his bowels moved in fear,
and how only adrenalin and faith
pulled him through.

And because heroes know the truth,
we don't feel all that heroic.

I remember in school when they talked about how to make the blade of a sword stronger. They would stick the blade into the fire to heat it and then take it out and hammer it again and again. I've come to believe this is what grief can do as well. It has thrown me into the fire of sorrow each day. It has beaten me senseless with the knowing that you are gone. But I am still here. Oh, I know I'm not a pretty sight right now, but I am still standing. Often I'm on my knees, but that is a standing of its own, too.

I am stronger than I ever thought I could be.

15

Night Stalker

The night has become a different place for me since you left. Once a time for cuddling, sleep, and rest, grief has stolen the night as well. In fact, the night has become his domain more than the day, for there are few distractions to keep him at bay. I stalk him, too. We are co-conspirators in sorrow.

HOLY COMMUNION

The house and I
took communion tonight
as if it were our last supper together.

And I walked its hallowed halls alone,
halls made sacred by the love we shared,
love that forswore all others.

I listened to the noises a house makes in the night,
like a great ship keening in the waves
and I wondered if Noah, too, listened in the night as I do.

And like Noah, I, too, have faith in the covenant
that someday we will be together again,
and I watch for the dove,
and the rainbow.

But tonight, I walk these halls,
my bare feet treading softly upon the carpet,
remembering the love that sheltered us here.

And I wonder, if I leave this house
will you know where to find me
to come sit on the edge of my bed when I cry?

Or will you wander these halls, alone and forlorn
as I do tonight, waiting for me to return ...

THE NIGHT IS FOR TEARS

The morning breaks and day begins,
a time for pouring cheerios and buttering toast,
and slipping into the shower and putting on face.

The first bell rings and work begins,
a time for conjugating verbs, correcting spelling,
and telling students for the millionth time why they can't
turn work in late.

The lunch bell rings,
time for nibbling tuna sandwiches, listening to
the gossip of the lunch room and complaints about this
year's freshmen.

The afternoon drags by,
time for correcting papers, emailing parents,
and gathering up the day.

The ride home begins,
time for running the gauntlet, walking the plank,
a half-mile of unimproved country road
that leads to a house where nobody's home,
where darkness falls like a velvet cloak

Time to let the tears fall, little pin-pricks
of blood from the wounds of the day,
like picking up the phone to call you,
then suddenly remembering you're not there.

Darkness deepens into night,
time to crawl into bed, where missing you
is all I can think of

Time to let the tears fall until I
am strong enough to let you go
and weak enough to sleep.

It is time for night,
and the night is for tears.

16

The Body Snatcher

Grief is a sneaky bastard. He is not satisfied with stealing happiness, joy, and memories. No, he wants it all. Lock, stock, and body. If you're not careful, he will get it, too. I discover that grief eats at you like a flesh-eating bacteria. My doctor warns me about broken-heart syndrome and writes me a scrip to keep me safe. *Too late*, I want to scream. *Thanks*, I whisper instead.

A BROKEN TICKER

I go and he listens
With his little scope
Placed on my chest

He nods his head
Eyebrows askew
Yes, I hear it
There is a sound

A wild thumping,
A pounding that
Doesn't belong

So with little stickies
All over my chest

He sends me home
To monitor the beats

And I walk the stairs
And sweep the floor,
Do all the things
I used to do
When you were here,
When our hearts beat as one,

And the little monitor
Attached to my hip
Begins to ping and to blip,
Its light gone wild,
Warning! Warning!
It shouts on its little graph

And I haven't the heart to
Tell him, with his seven years
Of medical school, and
All his medical degrees
Pinned to the walls of
His fancy new office

"What's the matter, mister?
Haven't you ever seen a
Broken heart before?"

17

Wakeup Call—2:00 A.M.

I don't tell the doctor about the wails at night. About how I hide in the small bathroom upstairs and sit on the floor and wail. So how could he predict a weakness in the throat, one that would explode one night? Blood pours out of my nose, but the blood down my throat is different. It's like a faucet has been turned on. My daughter calls for an ambulance. In the emergency room, she tells me, "I've already lost my dad. I don't want to lose you, too."

It's a wake-up call, I think.

Five Months in Hell

I chose the small bathroom
to better contain my sorrow.
On its floor, I sat and wailed
horrible, gut-wrenching wails
that ricocheted off the walls.

Until the walls began to tremble
and split like a great earthquake
had them by the tail.

The tears ran in torrents down my cheeks,
swirled down the shower drain, then overflowed
and followed the studs down to the
foundation, soaking the ground until
it became a bog of sorrow, swelling and lifting
the house from its foundation with
a horrific groan.

At five months, the tears became blood, and
I discovered that you don't have to stay in hell,
because you can carry it with you.

So I left the bathroom a bloody mess,
with its wail torn walls and its
tear mucked drain,
and now I travel the streets
like any ordinary person.

But if I were you,
I wouldn't want to be around
when all hell breaks loose.

18

Oobla-Dee, Oobla-Da . . .

For a while, life seems suspended in time. I am involved with the details of death: legal papers, funeral planning, social security, insurance, DMV. It's like driving along and suddenly your wheel gets caught in a deep rut, and you sit there, tire spinning wildly but getting nowhere. I am stuck in the business of loss.

Then, just as suddenly, the tire finds traction, and life goes on. I am shocked at first. My friends go home to their husbands, their normal lives. But what do I go on to? My life is stuck in the past. Friends are quick to say, "Oh, but you have your memories." This is true, of course, but in the beginning, memories are not what they might think. Memories are like razorblades. Instead of bringing me comfort, they sharpen the pain of what I have lost. I avoid them. Try to think of anything else but you. It doesn't work very well. I think of you, and it feels as if my heart bleeds with every thought. I find joy in nothing.

One day, though, I step outside to get the mail, and there, in the flowerbed, a tiny, yellow flower has pushed its way through the ground. I stoop to examine it. It is delicate, beautiful. I am shocked by that thought. For these past months, nothing has pierced my gloom. But this tiny flower makes me smile. I recognize beauty again. The world goes on. Not the world I have known, but a world nonetheless. There is beauty in this new world. I have just witnessed it. Felt it. My heart feels different. Lighter. Hopeful.

I have had, as my high school French teacher would say, an "attitude adjustment." I decide to stop fighting the memories. On the one year anniversary of your death, I pull out the DVD a friend made of your

Celebration of Life. I grab a box of tissues and sit cross-legged in your chair. I watch and listen to friends tell their favorite stories about you. How you made up the bunks for your sailing buddies, knowing they all had a few too many drinks and would need a place to crash. The kindness you showed a client who was suffering through a divorce. The stilts you made for the neighbors' kids. The tales go on and on. I sob, and laugh, and grieve. It is a different kind of grief now. It feels somehow cleansing.

I still cry when I think of you, of some silly little thing you did, or something we did together. But it feels different now. There is a joy in the memory, and a thankfulness for having had you at all.

Life goes on.

Memories become sweeter.

THE INCREDIBLE SWEETNESS OF LOVE

There is nothing like the sweetness of love.
Not infatuation, because that is just hormones,
and that doesn't last.

Not romance, because that is different from love.
Romance is flowers, and Saturday night dates,
and love notes and such ... all good things mind you,
but romance is only what leads up to love.
Love is in the little things, and by being in the little things,
it becomes the biggest thing of all.
Love is walking through the hardware store holding hands
even after 32 years.
It is feeling your back against mine as we sleep.

It is fixing your coffee in the morning, because it's
the one little thing I can do for you each day.
Love is covering you up after you've fallen asleep
on the couch for the third night in a row.

Love is making your sandwich and you telling me
that my sandwiches taste so much better than the ones
that you make, and then your smile when I tell you
that's because mine are made with love.

Love is me telling you I need the perfect little shelf
to go right here, and then hearing you whistle
in your workshop as you putter away making it for me.

Love is having a squabble, and then seeing you come
up the drive on your motorcycle with my favorite 32 ounce
Diet-Pepsi from S & K balanced on the seat between your legs.

Love is standing at the fireplace each morning, giving each
other the best bear-hugs in the world,
then putting on my lipstick and kissing you all over
your face, leaving my lip-prints and telling you that I'm marking
my territory so other women will know you belong to me,
and it is your grin in reply.

Love is surprising you on Valentine's Day by showing up at
your office in a trench-coat and heels to spend the day with you,
and then your look of surprise and unadulterated joy when I take
off the trench coat . . .

Love is driving to work in the morning, watching you ahead of
me on your motorcycle, then passing each other and smiling and
waving
and saying "I love you," and then, at the stoplight, me jumping
out of the car and running up to you, tilting your head back and
plastering a big kiss on your face, and us laughing as the guys
in the pickup next to us give you the big "thumbs-up."

Love is a billion, no, a trillion, little moments of joy so sweet
that, pulled into one life, create this extraordinary thing called
love.

And I think of a sign I saw today that said,
"Once in a while, in an ordinary life, you get a fairytale."

And I will miss you ever after.

19

Every Precious Little Thing

I didn't realize this at first, but in losing you I lost our history, that person who I could turn to and say, "remember when . . ."—and we would both end up laughing at an old memory. It feels like being lost in a strange city, and I can't remember who I am, and no one recognizes or remembers me. I didn't realize it at first, but in losing you, I lost myself as well.

As time grows longer from when I could see you and touch you, I sometimes feel as though I can't even imagine you in my mind, and it frightens me. When this happens, I get our big picture album, sit cross-legged on the floor with it, and pore over the pictures. I touch your image with my fingertips and try to pull you back into my memory. This comforts me. It helps me to know I can find you again and keep your face in my mind's eye. The pictures take me to a moment in time when we were together. They connect me to our lost history, to our memories. I take from each picture a moment in time, and I relive it, every precious little thing.

LIGHT IS FALLING

"Wake up!" you whisper, patting me gently on the shoulder.
"There's a meteor shower—come watch with me."

I tumble out of bed and we make our way downstairs.
On the lawn you have a thrown a blanket,
and we lie on our backs, spreading our arms
like snow angels and looking up at the sky.

Meteors spill from the night, little surprises of light,
silent, arching, flittering
We, too, are silent, expectant,
the night a canvas filled with splashes of wonder.

The dew-tipped grass seeps through the blanket,
making me shiver, and you pull me into your embrace,
"They are dying," you say, as I snuggle into your warmth.
"Friction causes them to burn, and the light is their last glow
before they turn to dust."

You point to a star twinkling in the night,
"And there we are," you say.
Love's gravitational pull joined us at the core,
we are a fragile supernova,
burning brightly toward our dust,

And suddenly I see the truth,
how fleeting life is,
how quickly it burns through the night,
always, light is falling.

An urgency awakens in me,
a voice that whispers, "Hurry!"

And I know that when you wake me
in the night, and say "Come,"
I will take your hand,
and we will run toward the light,
because always,
light is falling,

light is falling.

The Secret of Stars

When you are lost and alone,
stars reach down and take
your hand and say look,
touch the North star,
center yourself,
find Orion's Belt,
order your world.

Then they caress your cheek with
their cool gaze and go
quietly into the night.

Stars are constant.
During the day, when we
forget their glow,
they watch us still,
hovering, fussing, worrying, loving us
beyond measure.

And when they are worn and frazzled from care,
they burn white hot and are born again
in the heavens,
and we are comforted by their presence.

Stars know what we forget,
even though we burn to dust,
we are born again in the heavens
and find solace in the night.

Sweet Talkin' Man

Sometimes I just get a yen
for some of your slow southern drawl,
so sweet I can taste it right on the
tip of my tongue,

and I yearn to hear you call me "sugar"
just one more time,
punctuated by that shit-faced grin
of yours, letting me know I'm in
for all kinds of trouble

before "darlin'" ever slips
out, making me all warm
and melted on the inside like
honey on a biscuit . . .

THE OLD MUD HOLE

We were supposed to grow old together, you and I,
and we would sit on the porch and watch the day begin,
you drinking your coffee, me reading my morning paper, and we
would laugh together as time took its toll.

You would groan about your receding hairline,
and I would tell you, "there's just more of you to kiss,"
then I would groan about my bulging middle,
and you would say, "there's just more of you to hug."

And we would wallow in our enjoyment of one another
like two pigs wallow in the mud on a lazy afternoon,
knowing that no matter how crazy life can get,
it wouldn't really matter because at the end of the day,
it was just you and me in the mud-hole together.

There was a communion of sorts in our silence on the porch,
an understanding of the beauty of our love and its promise,
the promise to never forsake one another,
to hold each other dear no matter what the circumstance.

A sense of shared history, both joy and sorrow,
bound our hearts together, gave us comfort and peace
together, our little mud-hole felt like home.

20

Bumps in the Road

Life gets better. Easier. I can laugh again. But at any given moment, in the oddest of places, I am brought to my knees, missing you so much that I can hardly bear it. Last night on the Internet, a picture of an artist lounging casually at home surfaces and there you are. My breath catches in my throat in recognition. You are there in the way he sits in the chair, his ankle propped across his knee, his shirt sleeves rolled up. How many times have I seen you like this? It is a flashback. Unexpected. Aching.

DEAR MYSPACE

I want to report this image,
it claims to be a photo, but anyone can clearly see it
is a poem draped sensuously
across a chair,

legs and arms all sinewy
and lean,
white pants resting against
cool skin,
pressing against hot blood,
rushing against wild bones,
straining against desire and lust,

all concealed neatly behind
the unconcerned stare of
chocolate brown eyes
hot as Mexican cocoa.

Just look at those obscene
feet, each toe-knuckle a
pearl of undiscovered desire
hidden discreetly beneath the
pounding of his untamed heart.

Even in still-life, it is
clear he moves with the rhythm
of the bard, each sigh a sonnet,
every embrace a couplet
ending in rhyme and reason.

And I know this poem like
the back of my eyes,
and I see him in my dreams
and I taste him in my words.

We spent our youth counting
out syllables and parsing out
rhyme and called it love,

and now . . .
he pretends to be nothing more
than a black and white image
on some dated page.

MySpace,
I want to report this image!

These bumps in the road occur less and less often, but when they
happen, I give in to the moment. I miss you. I cry. I tell you, "I will always
love you." And then, I go on. I am strong enough to do that now.

21

Follow My Finger . . .

You know when you go to the eye doctor and he holds his index finger in front of your face and says, "follow my finger"? He then moves it left to right, then right to left. If you do it correctly, your eyes are in good shape. If not, well, it's glasses for you, bucko.

There I am, sitting in the chair,
the chart on the wall across the room,

E

HN

DFN

UZOTF

DFBPTH

Suddenly, I get it. It's all about **FOCUS**.

I think it's that way with grief, too. Or, rather, it's that way with surviving it. It's all about focus. Where am I focused? Am I focused on what I've lost? Or am I focused on what I've had? This is what I know. When I am focused on what I've lost, I can't see beyond my tears. I can't function. I can't do much of anything.

When I focus on what I have had, the beautiful and loving relationship with you, the many years we had together, the beautiful girls we brought into this world, I know I am truly blessed. How can I complain? I know what we have never seems like it is enough, but I have been blessed with so much. I almost feel it is an insult to God to continue to wallow in my grief. There is a time to mourn, and there is a time for joy.

I know this. I have many days of happiness, and then I jump back in the wallowing pit. I can't seem to let it go. But the wallowing gets further and further apart, and the moments of joy last longer and longer.

It's all about focus. I might be myopic with my grief, but my distance vision for joy is getting better. I just have to remind myself.

Focus. Focus. Focus.

MYOPIA

My grief is like an old scab,
picked at and worried until
it falls away, revealing the
bloody mush hiding just
beneath the surface.

I wish I could leave it alone,
but old memories and longing
prickle and ache until
my fingers, too, are bloodied
by the pain, even though
I scold them and tell them,
again and again,
"Leave it alone, leave it
alone."

22

Just Weird Thoughts

In spite of all good effort, sometimes weird thoughts just creep into my brain. At first, they made me feel like I was going crazy, but now I consider them grief "bubbles" just rising to the surface now and again.

Nothing to worry about.

OXYMORON

. . . filled to the brim
with the
oxymoronic
notion that emptiness means nothing, when
it actually means everything . . .

as in realizing that inside
nothingness
resides all that is
missing,

so, in effect,
when you are feeling
empty,
you are actually filled
to the brim with those
things that you are missing . . .

stuffed to the gills with
them, until you find it
impossible to breathe,
or to think,
or to move

and the worst part is
that you know, if they meant nothing,

then you wouldn't be filled to the
brim with
emptiness . . .

Capiche?

LOST AND FOUND

Lately, my head has become
a repository for the lost and found.
My mind finds a thought or two,
makes a mental note to remember them later,
then just as quickly, loses them in the rubble of my brain.

Yet, useless information, trivial pursuits,
bob to the surface like dead fish,
I keep batting them away, and
others pop up taking their place.

Someone needs to claim these useless thoughts,
take them to the needy, those who haven't a thought in their heads.
Let them find a use for Elvis' song "Wooden Heart."
Where did that come from anyway?

Or give them that useless old geometry theorem that
keeps rattling around in my brain.
It's like my brain knows there's a problem it needs to solve
and is searching all its memory banks.

But the problem is, the brain is used to keeping track of
thoughts,
filing them away for later use,
but in matters of the heart, the brain has greater trouble
trying to sort out such things as,
"My legs ache because you're gone,
There's a pain in my arm because you're not here to hold."

It's like you've short-circuited my system,
and my brain keeps misfiring, trying to get back in rhythm.
It hardly functions as a brain anymore
I've been shuffled off to the bowels of some derelict building,
and someone's tacked a hand-printed sign on my forehead,
"She's lost; we found her,"
and I'm waiting for someone to claim what's left of me.

23

Let's Pretend

I do my best to live in the reality that is my life now. But today, on the drive to work, I just don't want to be there anymore. I want my world righted again, like it was when you were here.

I think back to when we were kids and we used to play all sorts of games. One of the most fun was "Let's Pretend." We would pretend we were astronauts in a spaceship we made from a mattress box. We laid it flat on the ground and crawled inside. We cut windows into the end and sides, covering them with paper that we had drawn stars on. We spent hours inside that spaceship, flying all over our universe.

Sometimes we played house in the room in the barn that my uncle Charles fixed for us. There was an old mattress on the floor for a bed, a peach-box nailed to the wall for cupboards, an old table and chairs, and the best thing was a wall phone made out of an old barn-door handle. We had many conversations with important people on that phone, and many slumber parties on that old mattress.

But as we grew up, we played "Let's Pretend" less and less until, finally, the reality of the adult world engaged us completely. I've lived in this adult world for a long time, fully accepting the responsibilities and the realities it forces on me. But today, I played pretend once more.

Today dawned, cool and grey, and the mollygrubs got me. So on the way to work I played "Let's Pretend." Just for today, I decided that this time without you has just been one long nightmare. Today, the nightmare was over, and I pretended that you weren't gone.

You were in your office, working, and I would call you today and we would chat. After school I would go to your office, and when I opened the door and peeked in, you would look up from your computer. Your face would light up when you saw me, and your sweet grin would make my heart beat fast, just like it always did. I would sit in the chair in front of your desk, and we would talk about our day, and you would putz around, shutting things down so you could take me to dinner.

And just for today, you wouldn't really be gone, and my heart wouldn't be broken. I would tell you about this terrible dream I had, and you would hug me tight and tell me it was only a bad dream, because you would never, ever leave me. And I would hug you back and say I know, you wouldn't because you always promised me.

And just for a few moments, I was a kid again, and life didn't suck, and life didn't end on a Thursday afternoon in April. And just for a few moments, I was the happiest girl in the whole wide world.

Because just for a few moments, I could pretend.

24

Saving Grace

I'm not sure how other people survive this. I only know, from my own experience, how I get through each day.

Faith.

.

I look at the period I've typed above, and it is so tiny. In the context of the letters on the page, it seems almost insignificant, yet it can control powerful thoughts, change purpose or intention, and create meaning out of a chaos of words.

I think of the mustard seed, insignificant next to the period. Yet faith as small as that can control the direction of a soul, change the purpose or intention of a heart, and create meaning out of the chaos of loss.

Faith as small as a mustard seed can save you. It saved me.

Love is really faith
and faith is believing,
believing is a choice,
and I choose to
believe in love,
which is really faith,
and faith
brings peace.

25

Epiphany

O ne night, during my wailing session in the bathroom, I cried out to God in agony. I felt His presence there with me. It suddenly came to me that God understands my suffering because He suffered this for me. While my sweet husband appeared to have died peacefully in his sleep, God's son was tortured, spat upon, and hung to suffer on a cross. How could God bear such agony? Although I knew this to be true from the age of eight, until this moment, I never understood the magnitude of God's loss and the great love it took for Him to do this. In my suffering, I finally understood God's suffering. That night, in the small confines of my bathroom, we held each other and wept.

April is the cruelest month, breeding
Lilacs out of the dead land, mixing
Memory and desire, stirring
Dull roots with spring rain.
                                                    —T.S. Eliot

EPIPHANY

It's funny, or maybe not, how old poets
from your past come back to haunt
you when you wish they'd stayed
dead and holed up in some ancient
text, escaping only to torment
some new frosh in English Lit,
40 years your junior,
with poem structure, notes on
allusion, and frantic 2:00 A.M.
soul-searching of "What the hell does
this line mean?" before the 1:00 P.M.
exam the next afternoon.

But like it or not, when you're
all comfortable and middle-aged,
unsuspecting and vulnerable,
that line tracks you down, and
like a heat-seeking missile, it
demands full atonement for
earlier sins of misunderstanding.

In a come to Jesus moment,
understanding washes over you, and
you ache to run back into
that professor's class waving
your arms frantically to warn them.

We were fools; it's not the structure, or the
line breaks, or the poet's tone,
those are only words on a page,
and some professor's lofty foray into academia.
It's not that at all . . .

"April is the cruelest month,"
a line mocked by our youth and
innocence, becomes poetry only
by the living of the line.

Oh, you can dance around it in your youth,
tossing interpretations like kites into the wind, but
once the land lays waste, and
your loved one turns to dust by
summer's heat, then winter's frost,

only then, when spring pokes her
head up in April, is the line made real,
only then does it bloom into understanding,
mixing memory of what has been
with the desire of wanting
what cannot be again.

And the juxtaposition of spring flowers
against the death of hope,
sharpens understanding.

It is through faith that I survive. It is through faith that I know I will
see Tony again one day. It is faith that keeps me from destroying myself in
this grief. It is through faith that I know that God will bring joy into my
life again. I know that this suffering will pass, but it is up to me to choose
to let it go.

God Has the Last Word

After 57 years, the Night had
had enough and told the Day so
in no uncertain terms.

Of course, Day would have none of
it, and so a fight ensued, causing quite
a ruckus in all parts of the neighborhood.

And they carried on for months about
who was to have you, or who had
higher claim, until God intervened,
did a giant smack-down,

and said, "Listen, you two, I put you onto
this earth and I can take you
off," and they sputtered and fumed
and tried to settle down.

But as soon as His back was turned, they
started again, until He returned to the
fray in a thunder of rain, sighing, "All right,
already, just plead your case."

And so the Day began, "Well, you see,
God, I shine on his face. I put the auburn
in his hair. I give him light to see
his way. I put the twinkle in his eye."

"True, true," God said. "And you?" He
asked, nodding at Night.

"Well, Sir, I bring slumber for his dreams.
I bring moonlight to guide his path. I show him the
North Star so he can find his way. I give him
rest from the worries of the day."

God nodded appreciatively.

And, of course, you know me,
not one to walk away from a fight,
I stepped up timidly (I mean,
this was God after all).

"And what do you want?" He asked.

"Well, God," I began. "You see, I've loved him for 32 years.
Some of those years were pretty tough, but
I remembered what I promised You about
'through sickness and health,' and all that.
Of course I didn't really understand about that
'til death do us part' clause until now.

"But I'd really like to keep him, Sir. You see,
our hearts have become one,
like You said they would, and it's
really going to hurt if You take him away."

"Yeah, yeah, yeah, it's all about you," God scowled.
"But what did you do for him?"

I thought about it long and hard. "Well, Sir," I answered.
"I held his hand in the daylight, and we faced the hardships
of the world together. I kissed each freckle the Day
placed on his face and told him a reason for loving him for
every one. I made him coffee every day. I carried his babies and
gave him laughter and joy. In the Night, I slept in his arms and
promised I would love him forever."

"Whoa, those are some good reasons, too," God said. He began
to squirm on His throne. He began to wring His great hands.
He looked at the three of us, "Who do you think I am? Solomon?"
He asked.

He jumped up and began to pace, and suddenly stopped, slapping His forehead. "Wait a minute—I'm God!" He exclaimed. He turned to us, beaming.

"Look! I've got a plan. We'll share him.
I will bring him home with Me so he can rest.
Day, you can shine on the world he saw, the places he went.
He'll be there in every sunbeam you send down. Night, you can place his dreams in the moon, and he can shine down on the world at night with you. It'll be like he never left."

God turned to me, "What are you sniveling about now?"
I couldn't help it then. The tears gushed like Noah's flood, and I stood there, slinging snot and bawling right there in front of God.

"It's just that I'm going to miss him so much," I cried.

God reached out and placed His great hand on my shoulder. As He looked at me, His big eyes softened.

"But, you'll see him again," He said.

"I promise."

26

Life After Death

FINDING MY WAY

Like a newly blinded person,
I probe the ground ahead with
a tentative toe, pushing gently
to see if it will hold my weight.

My steps are small,
and the going is slow,
some days I don't move at all,
I just stand, dumbfounded
by where I am,
and why . . .

There is no compass
to show the way,
no hand to slip
mine into that will lead,
so that I might follow.

There is no recognition,
or even intuition for which
path I should take,
only a vast expanse of
empty road ahead.

And I,
without you,
am lost in
the wilderness.

But faith is stronger than fear, and
even at a snail's pace,
I move on,
only to discover that
losing you has made me strong,
resilient,
brave.
So I thrust out my chin,
stiffen my spine,
and step ahead, knowing
that if I should fall,
I can pick myself up, because
I learned that from
losing you.

LOVE'S OLD SWEET SONG

I learned so much from loving Tony. I learned that life is too short to be sad. Every day that I have, I want to be happy. He taught me that love is a joyful adventure. I want to have that again. My sister and I were discussing my future, and she reminded me that, if I live as long as my dad and mom, I could have 20 or more years to enjoy a new relationship. Even if I only had, say, 5 or 10 years, wouldn't I want them to be happy, too? Tony would want me to be happy. I'm sure of that.

Somehow though, it makes me feel weird, like I'm being unfaithful by thinking of another relationship. And even if I do, how long before it feels right? The books tell you not to make any big changes for a year. I think that sounds reasonable. The first year is pretty messed up. I could barely change my clothes. Not a very good time to be thinking of a new relationship.

So I gave it a year. But I have to tell you, I was really lonely. I was so happily married. I was not so happily single. I will say this though, I finally came to a place of peace with being single. I enjoyed being in charge of the remote. I enjoyed doing whatever I wanted at the end of the day. I just enjoyed being married more. I love being with someone I love. I like doing things together.

But how do you meet somebody when you are 56 years old? I love them, but from a dating aspect, my friends are pretty useless. They are all married. Their friends are married, too. The one time a friend tries to set me up it is a disaster. Most of the people my age at church are married. No luck there.

I decide to try the Internet. E-Harmony lets me down. I think I am too specific in my answers, and the two or three they match me with are a no go. I try Match.com. I like this one. You get to look at pictures and bios and screen them yourself. It's sort of like shopping. No, not sort of, I guess it really is shopping for a relationship. I connect and email back and forth with some men who are in nearby towns. I meet a couple of them. I'm way too frantic and nervous. I realize I don't really want this. It's too in my face. Too close.

I search in other states. Colorado looks like a nice place. I find one man who has a great smile. Dave. He lost his wife Norma to cancer a year before I lost Tony. We email for several months. He sends me his phone number and says to call if I want. I wait. Finally, one night, I call his number. I'm so nervous I can hardly talk. But, soon, just like in our emails, we are chatting away like old friends. I give him my number. We talk a lot. Months go by. He asks if we can meet. I am petrified. One night, I say, "Okay, let's meet."

We decide that he will fly to California and stay in a local hotel. Before he comes I turn into a detective. I call the bank where he says he works. I ask for him; he answers and I hang up. Okay, he really works there. I go to Whitepages.com and check for his phone number. Yes, he lives where he says he does. My friend suggests a background check to see if he has any felonies, but when I tell her he is an investment officer at the bank handling stocks, she says he couldn't do that if he had any felonies. So far so good.

He comes to see me. The rest, you might say, is history. For the next year, we support the airlines, flying back and forth to see each other. Eventually, we decide the time apart is too long, too lonely.

On September 24, 2008, three years and five months after becoming a widow, I become a wife. I like it. A lot.

HOPE

What does "hope" look like?
This I know.

It is . . .

brown eyes smiling at me
from a photograph,

a new message popping up
in my "inbox,"

late night phone calls,
laughter, and, sometimes tears,
shared across the miles,

feeling seventeen again,
acting goofy and silly, and
not caring because
there is such fun in the nonsense,

breathing in and out
for the first time in months
without pain clutching at my heart,

replacing pain with laughter
and sorrow with possibility,

looking forward instead of back.

It is . . .

reaching out and embracing another heart
that is embracing hope too . . .

So, here I am, making new memories with a man I love completely. A man who loves me back in a way that makes me feel whole again. I think of one of the things he used to say when we were dating, and it makes me smile—"Pick me, pick me."

The SPCA of Love

Like two pound puppies, tails wagging,
noses pressed against the fence,
we wait for love,

someone to take us home, scratch
that itch behind our ears
and rub our bellies,

someone who will overlook that
in doggie years,
we're no longer puppies,

our coats tinged with gray,
even bare in some places,
jowls a little droopy,
our bark more bluff than bite.

So we search their eyes,
with a silent promise
not to chew on their best shoes,
and to snuggle against their backs
as they sleep,

and, if given the chance
to be faithful and true,
as good dogs are known to be,
just to hear one more time,
"Good dog! Good dog!"

and as the puppies romp around us
in their cuteness of youth,
we wait at the fence and pray,
"Pick me! Pick me!"

A Few Last Thoughts . . .

As I sit here writing this now, I know that in the early days and months of losing Tony I never could have imagined that I would know joy and love like this again. As I observed others in the grief groups early on, I never saw the same struggle that I was going through. It made me feel as though something was terribly wrong with me. Why was I suffering so when others seemed to bear it better than me?

What I've come to understand is that they probably didn't. This kind of pain is hidden and kept under wraps. It's as if we are embarrassed by such strong emotions. But, if we can't show it to the world, at least we can show it honestly in a book. If I could have read it somewhere, just to know that someone else suffered like I did, it would have helped me understand that I was not alone. I was not crazy. I was simply grief-stricken.

Looking back over my writings, sometimes they appear to me to be jumbled and without a coherent order. Yet that is how my grief evolved. At times it seemed wildly out of control, but even that had its purpose. Grief gave me just what I could handle at the moment. By doing this, He kept me from falling deep into Alice's rabbit hole without a way of climbing out again.

Your grief may not look like mine. It is your grief, and it will be what you need it to be. I turned to writing to survive. You may choose something else as your weapon against grief. But I want you to know this: Although it will hurt like hell, it will get better.

I promise.

Acknowledgments

Even though it might have felt in the beginning that I was alone in my struggle with grief, there are countless family and friends who touched my heart with their concern and thoughtful acts. My daughters Shea Taylor Klinghoffer and Brie Taylor, close friends Alice Keeler, Janet and Bob Groth, Janice Noga-Speace, Karen Walker, and Sharon and Gary Motsenbocker loved and supported me through those first hours, days, and weeks. My friends Marilyn and Keith Schwemmer provided support, often in the wee hours of the night. CUSD administrators Norm Anderson and Dr. Cheryl Rogers provided strength and support in that first difficult hour. The faculty and staff at Clovis High School, a family within itself, created a beautiful Celebration of Life for Tony, with Wendy Karsevar and Bobbie Bass making a memorable music and video presentation for the event.

Janice Stevens and the members of my writing group, Valley Writers and Artists, encouraged me to share my story, with Anne Biggs, Diane Skouti, Gary Walker, Kathy Gorman, Lee Self, and Annalisa Havlik, my friend in the grieving process, providing extraordinary commentary. A special thank you to Central Coast Writers for the Lillian Dean Award and Kent Sorsky for supporting my work.

Thank you also to the Clovis Police Department and the Fresno County Coroner's Office for their professional and gentle approach to such a loss.

I want to especially acknowledge my students, whose love and compassion during my return to work gave me purpose and direction. Your extra efforts on my behalf only increased my respect for teenagers and what you bring to the world around you. To Andrew Peralta, Josh Esparza, Ariana Sanchez, Jaipriya Kaur, and Temma Curry—a special thank you.

Finally, I want to thank my husband, Dave. His love and support show me daily that love is big enough for yesterday and tomorrow.